Chemicals in Action

Metals

Chris Oxlade

Heinemann
LIBRARY

www.heinemann.co.uk/library
Visit our website to find out more information about **Heinemann Library** books.

To order:
 Phone 44 (0) 1865 888066
 Send a fax to 44 (0) 1865 314091
Visit the Heinemann Bookshop at www.heinemann.co.uk/library to browse our catalogue and order online.

First published in Great Britain by Heinemann Library, Halley Court, Jordan Hill, Oxford OX2 8EJ, a division of Reed Educational and Professional Publishing Ltd. Heinemann is a registered trademark of Reed Educational & Professional Publishing Limited.

OXFORD MELBOURNE AUCKLAND JOHANNESBURG BLANTYRE
GABORONE IBADAN PORTSMOUTH NH (USA) CHICAGO

Designed by Tinstar Design (www.tinstar.co.uk)
Illustrations by Jeff Edwards.
Originated by Ambassador Litho Ltd.
Printed in China by Wing King Tong.

ISBN 0 431 136017 (hardback)   ISBN 0 431 136084 (paperback)
06 05 04 03 02   07 06 05 04 03
10 9 8 7 6 5 4 3 2   10 9 8 7 6 5 4 3 2 1

British Library Cataloguing in Publication Data
Oxlade, Chris
Metals. - (Chemicals in action)
1.Metals - Juvenile literature
I.Title
546.3

Acknowledgements
The Publishers would like to thank the following for permission to reproduce photographs:
Andrew Lambert pp20, 26, 32, Holt Studios p15, Paul Brierly p34, Peter Gould p22, Robert Harding pp9, 16, 18, 28, 36, 39, Roger Scruton pp17, 38, Science Photo Library pp4, 5, 6, 10, 12, 15, 19, 24, 33, 35, 37, Telegraph Colour Library p31, Trevor Clifford pp11, 13, 19, 25, 29.

Cover photograph reproduced with permission of Photodisc.

The Publishers would like to thank Dr Nigel Saunders for his assistance in the preparation of this book.

Every effort has been made to contact copyright holders of any material reproduced in this book. Any omissions will be rectified in subsequent printings if notice is given to the Publisher.

Contents

Words appearing in the text in bold, **like this**, are explained in the glossary.

Chemicals in action

What's the link between an artificial joint, a jet engine, a computer, a battery and a frying pan? The answer is **metals**. All these things are made of metals or work because of metals, or because of chemical reactions between metals. Our knowledge of how metals behave is used in choosing which metals to use to manufacture things, in engineering, in medicine and in recycling.

The study of metals is part of the science of chemistry. Many people think of chemistry as something that scientists study by doing experiments in laboratories full of test tubes and flasks of bubbling liquids. This part of chemistry is very important. It is how scientists find out what substances are made of and how they make new materials – but this is only a tiny part of chemistry. Most chemistry happens away from laboratories, in factories and chemical plants. It is used to manufacture an enormous range of items, such as synthetic fibres for fabrics, drugs to treat diseases, explosives for fireworks, solvents for paints, and fertilizers for growing crops.

The light, strong metal aluminium was used to make fuel tanks for the Arianne 5 *rocket.*

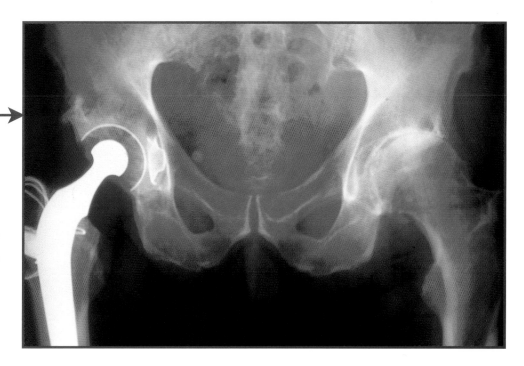

This X-ray shows an artificial ball-and-socket hip joint, made from corrosion-resistant metal.

About the experiments

There are several experiments in the book for you to try. Doing these will help you to understand some of the chemistry in the book. An experiment is designed to help solve a scientific problem. Scientists use a logical approach to experiments so that they can conclude things from the results of the experiments. A scientist first writes down a hypothesis, which he or she thinks might be the answer to the problem, then designs an experiment to test the hypothesis. He or she then writes down the results of the experiment and concludes whether the results show that hypothesis is true or not. We only know what we do about chemistry because scientists have carefully carried out thousands of experiments over hundreds of years.

Experiments have allowed scientists to discover many different metals, how metals behave in chemical reactions, and how to **extract** metals from the rocks of the Earth's crust.

Doing the experiments

All the experiments in this book have been designed for you to do at home with everyday substances and equipment. They can also be done in the school laboratory. Always follow the safety advice given with each experiment and ask an adult to help you when the instructions tell you to.

About metals

When you hear the word '**metal**' you probably think of something shiny and hard, such as knives and forks, jewellery, pots and pans, and tools. We make all these objects from metals because they have useful **properties**. For example, many metals are strong, can withstand heat and **conduct** electricity. Metals are also used on a much bigger scale: they make up structures such as skyscrapers and bridges, and machines such as trains and trucks.

Metals are found in rocks that make up the Earth's crust. Getting them out of the rocks and preparing them so that manufacturers can use them to make objects is a massive industry. Various **chemical reactions** are used to **extract** the metals from the rocks they are found in. Other chemical reactions change the metals when we use them. For example some metals, such as iron, are weakened when they react with gases in the air.

The fuselages and wings of airliners are made from aluminium. Some parts are made from strong aluminium alloys.

Metal elements

Metals used in metal objects are either pure metals or **alloys**. Pure metals contain only one sort of metal. Alloys contain a metal with other metals or **non-metals** added to it. When chemists talk about a metal, they mean a metal that is an **element**. An element is a substance made up of one type of **atom**, for example, the metal aluminium (used in kitchen foil) is made up of just aluminium atoms.

Metals are one of the two main groups of elements and they appear on the left-hand side of the periodic table. About three-quarters of all the elements are metals and they are identified by their properties, such as their shininess and ability to conduct electricity. The other group are the non-metals. A few elements have some of the properties of both metals and non-metals; they are called **metalloids** or semi-metals.

Most coins are made from hard-wearing alloys so that they last a long time in circulation.

Alloys

An alloy is a material that is made up of a **mixture** of two or more different metals, or a metal and one or more non-metals. They are made in chemical plants. Mixing different metals and non-metals produces alloys that have useful properties. For example, brass is an alloy of copper and zinc, and it is stronger than both metals and does not **corrode**.

Properties of metals

There are more than a hundred different **elements**, and each has **properties** that make it look, feel and behave differently to the others. Each one is made up of a different type of **atom**.

The elements are divided into two main groups, **metals** and **non-metals**, according to their properties. About three-quarters of the elements are metal. They all have similar properties to each other and they are described as metallic. They look and behave in a similar way. Non-metals are elements that do not have the properties of metals.

This table shows the properties of metals and non-metals:

Metals	Non-Metals
Mostly solids	Mostly gases at room temperature
Hard, shiny and **malleable**	Weak, dull and brittle when solids
Good **conductors** of electricity	Insulators (except graphite)
Good conductors of heat	Poor conductors of heat
High **melting** and **boiling points**	Low melting and boiling points
High **densities**	Low densities
Oxides are basic	Oxides are acidic

Inside a metal

All materials are made up of incredibly tiny **particles** called atoms, which are too small to see, even with the most powerful microscopes. An atom is made up of a central **nucleus** surrounded by particles called **electrons**. In a piece of metal, the atoms are arranged in neat rows and columns, and they are tightly packed together. Each atom is attached to the atoms around it by chemical **bonds** and this is why most metals are strong materials.

We make use of the properties of metals in structures such as bridges and skyscrapers. The frame of this bridge tower is made of strong metal girders, while the roadway is supported by strong, but flexible, cables.

Shine and colour

All metals have shiny surfaces when they are freshly cut or polished. Many metals lose their shininess after a while because the metal at the surface reacts with oxygen in the air, forming a layer of oxide. Some metals, such as gold, do not react with oxygen so they stay shiny, and are used for decorations such as jewellery. Most metals are grey or silvery in colour.

Changing shape

Metals are flexible, which means they can change shape slightly and return to their original shape. This is why springs are made of metal. Metals are also malleable, which means that a piece of metal can be hammered into a different shape without it snapping. Metals are also **ductile** and can be pulled thinner and longer without breaking.

Metal densities

Most **metals** have high **densities**; they are heavy for their size compared to other materials such as wood or plastic. Some metals are very dense, for example, a piece of tungsten the size of a large drinks bottle weighs as much as an average adult person! There are a few metals with very low densities, for example, sodium even floats on water.

Metal tracks carry electricity across this circuit board.

Metals and electricity

All metals allow electricity to pass through them, so we say they are good **conductors** of electricity. An electric current is made up of a moving electric **charge** and in a metal the charge is carried by **electrons**. Some electrons from each **atom** are free to move from atom to atom and they move through a piece of metal, carrying the charge. Metals such as iron, copper, aluminium and gold are used in electricity cables and in electrical circuits inside machines because they conduct the electricity.

In most **non-metals**, and in most **compounds**, the electrons cannot move, so they cannot conduct electricity.

Magnetic metals

A few metals are **magnetic**, which means that they are attracted to magnets and they can also be turned into magnets. For example, metal paper clips are attracted to a magnetic desk tidy. The most common magnetic metal is iron. The **alloy** steel is also magnetic because it is mostly iron. The two other main magnetic metals are nickel and cobalt. Magnetism is sometimes used in industry to sort metals during processing or recycling.

Radioactive metals

The **nucleus** of an atom is made up of **particles** called **protons** and **neutrons**. Some metals, such as uranium and plutonium, have a large nucleus in their atoms that contain hundreds of protons and neutrons. A large nucleus like this is quite unstable. Neutrons and protons often break away from it naturally, making it smaller and more stable. These metals are described as **radioactive** because when a nucleus breaks up it releases **radiation** in the form of invisible rays. Normally the new nucleus has fewer protons, so the atom of the original **element** has become an atom of a new, different element.

Experiment: Magnetic sorting

PROBLEM: How can we separate magnetic objects from a mixture of objects?

HYPOTHESIS: We can use one of the **properties** of iron, which is that it is a magnetic metal.

> **EQUIPMENT**
> iron or steel nails
> copper nails
> brass screws
> magnet

Experiment steps

1 Mix up some iron or steel nails with some copper nails and brass screws.

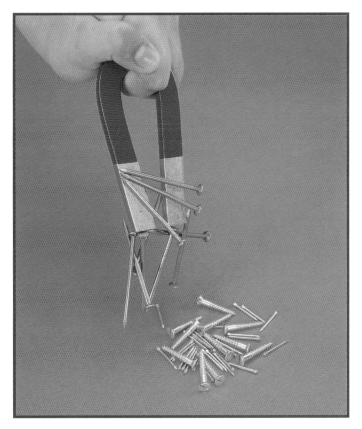

2 Move a magnet over the mixed nails and screws.

CONCLUSION: The iron is magnetic so the iron nails are attracted to the magnet. The copper nails and brass screws are left behind.

Metals and heat

All **metals** allow heat to flow through them. They are called good **conductors** of heat, which means that if you heat one part of a metal object, the heat spreads quickly to the other parts of the object. This **property** of metals has both advantages and disadvantages. Cooking pans are made of metal because they conduct heat from the stove to the food inside them, but if you have a pan that also has a metal handle, you have to lift it with a cloth to stop it burning your hands!

Metals are good conductors because their **atoms** are closely packed together and strongly joined. The atoms in every material always vibrate because they have heat energy. The hotter an object becomes, the faster its atoms vibrate because each one is getting more heat energy. When one part of a metal object is heated, the atoms in that part begin to vibrate faster because they are getting more energy. Some of this energy passes to the atoms next door, making them vibrate too, and gradually the energy spreads through the object.

When atoms get more energy and vibrate more, they take up a tiny bit more space. This is why all materials, including metals, expand (get bigger) slightly when they get hotter and contract (get smaller) slightly when they get cooler.

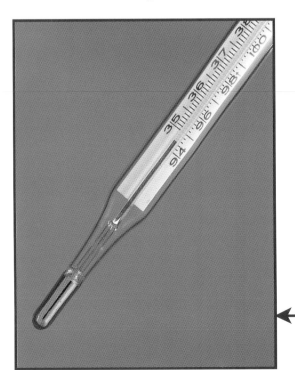

Melting and boiling points

All metals except mercury are solids at room temperature; this shows that they have high **melting points**. They also have high **boiling points**. For example, iron melts at 1535°C and boils at 2861°C. Metals have these high melting and boiling points because their atoms are strongly joined together. Metals with very high melting points are used to make objects that are used in very hot environments, such as inside jet engines.

Mercury trapped inside a thermometer expands when it gets warmer, indicating the temperature.

Experiment: Testing heat conduction

PROBLEM: Are metals better conductors of heat than plastics?

HYPOTHESIS: If heat spreads more quickly through metal than plastic, then it is a better heat conductor.

> **EQUIPMENT**
> garden peas
> petroleum jelly
> metal teaspoon
> plastic teaspoon
> mug

Experiment steps

1 Stick a pea to one end of each of the teaspoons using a small blob of petroleum jelly.

2 Ask an adult to pour hot (not boiling or steaming) water into the mug, and stand the teaspoons in it. Make sure that the peas stay out of the water.

3 Carefully observe the petroleum jelly and the peas, and note down the order in which the petroleum jelly melts and the peas fall.

CONCLUSION: The pea on the metal teaspoon fell first. This shows that the heat spread more quickly through the metal than the plastic. Metals are therefore the better conductors of heat.

Families of metals

All the **metals** in the periodic table are found on the left-hand side. They are put into groups of metals with similar **properties**. These groups are the **alkali** metals, the alkaline earth metals, the transition metals, and the poor metals. This chapter looks at each group and the most important metals in them.

The alkali metals

The metals in group 1 of the periodic table are called the alkali metals. They are lithium, sodium, potassium, rubidium, caesium and francium. They are called alkali metals because they react with water to form alkaline solutions. For example:

$$\text{sodium} + \text{water} \longrightarrow \text{sodium hydroxide} + \text{hydrogen}$$

$$2Na + 2H_2O \longrightarrow 2NaOH + H_2$$

All the alkali metals are strongly **reactive** and as you move down the group, the more strongly reactive they are. This means they are more likely to take part in **chemical reactions**. For example, lithium (at the top the group) fizzes slowly in cold water, but caesium (near the bottom of the group) catches fire instantly when it is exposed to cold air! Lithium and sodium have very low **densities** for metals and are very soft. All the alkali metals are silvery white in colour. Because these metals are so reactive, they are rarely used on their own, but they have many useful **compounds**.

The alkaline earth metals

The metals in group 2 of the periodic table are called the alkaline earth metals. They are beryllium, magnesium, calcium, strontium, barium and radium. They are called the alkaline earth metals because their compounds were first found in plant remains in soil. They also react with water to form alkaline solutions. For example:

$$\text{calcium} + \text{water} \longrightarrow \text{calcium hydroxide} + \text{hydrogen}$$

$$Ca + 2H_2O \longrightarrow Ca(OH)_2 + H_2$$

The alkali metal potassium reacts violently with water. The heat from the reaction ignites the hydrogen it produces.

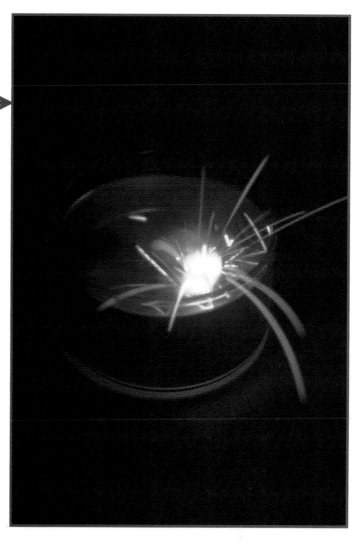

All the alkaline earth metals are very reactive and as you move down the group, the more strongly reactive they are. For example, magnesium (near the top of the group) will react quickly with steam, but only very slowly with water, and barium (near the bottom of the group) reacts quickly with water. Most of the alkaline earth metals are silvery white in colour. Like the alkali metals, they are rarely used alone but they do form some very important compounds.

The metals in groups 1 and 2 are also sometimes called the reactive metals.

Lettuce seedlings growing under lamps that are filled with sodium vapour, which gives out yellow-orange light.

The transition metals

Most **metals** are in a large group in the centre of the periodic table, sandwiched between groups 2 and 3. They are called the transition metals, and they are nearly all hard, strong metals with high **melting** and **boiling points**, and high **densities**. The most commonly used transition metals are iron, copper, zinc, gold and silver. Most of the other transition metals are very rare, and yet scientists and engineers have found uses for many of them. They are mixed with iron, steel or aluminium to make various **alloys** for engineering. Several, including palladium and platinum, are used as **catalysts** to speed up reactions in chemical plants.

Two groups of transition metals (sometimes called inner transition metals) do not fit neatly into the periodic table and are sometimes left out and shown in a separate block. They are called the lanthanides and the actinides, and many of them have only been made in the laboratory. Many, such as uranium, are also **radioactive**.

The transition metal chromium is used to make shiny parts for cars, and also to make stainless steel.

Gold and silver

Gold is the yellowy metal used to make jewellery and ornaments. It stays shiny because, unlike most other metals, it is very unreactive and so does not react with the air to form a layer of **oxide** that spoils the shine. Gold is quite soft, so it is normally alloyed with other metals (usually copper or silver) to stop it wearing away.

Silver is a white metal also used to make jewellery and ornaments. It gradually reacts with the air to form a brown layer of oxide, called tarnishing, which means that silver must be cleaned every few months. Many objects, including ornaments and cutlery, are silver plated, which means they are made of steel with a thin layer of silver on the outside.

Metals in your body

Your body needs some metals for it to grow and work properly. For example, about two per cent of your body is calcium, which is mostly in your bones. Our main source of calcium as we grow is milk. There are other metals in our bodies in tiny amounts, such as iron, zinc, magnesium and copper.

It is important to eat foods that contain these metals. Some people take tablets, such as iron tablets, to provide them with 'trace' metals, which are found in small amounts or 'traces' in the body.

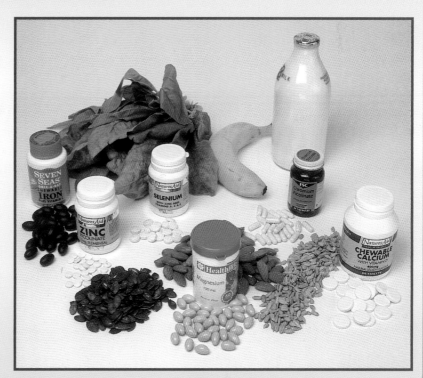

Iron and steel

Iron is a transition metal and one of the few **magnetic** metals. It is the most widely used metal of all. Pure iron is light in colour and quite soft. Sometimes it is made into decorative objects such as gates, railings and fire grates. Blacksmiths work with iron by heating it to make it softer and then hammering it into shape. Iron is also made into large machine parts, such as cylinder blocks in engines, and objects such as drain covers and pipes.

Decorative gates and railings are made of a type of impure iron called wrought iron.

Iron is often made into steel, which is an **alloy** of iron and carbon. Most steel contains about 99 per cent steel and about 1 per cent carbon. Steel is stronger and harder than pure iron, but less **malleable** and **ductile**. It is good for making objects that need to be strong and is used in thousands of different objects such as cars, ships, building frames, bridges, nails, screws and knives and forks.

Iron and steel rust quickly in damp air. You can find out how they are protected from rusting on page 28. Stainless steel is an alloy of steel that contains about ten per cent of chromium, another metal. The chromium means that it does not rust, even if it gets scratched.

You can find out how iron and steel are made on page 36.

Copper used for a decorative roof. The surface of the copper eventually turns green in damp air.

Copper

Copper is a soft, brown transition metal. It is a very good **conductor** of electricity, so it is used to make wires and cables. It is quite unreactive, so does not **corrode** in damp air like iron, and it is also easy to cut and shape. These **properties** make it ideal for manufacturing pipes for water supply and heating systems. Brass, used to make house fittings like door handles, locks and screws, is an alloy of copper and zinc. Many coins are made from copper alloys. The alloy keeps the colour of the copper, but it is harder – so coins made from alloys last longer than copper ones would.

Zinc

Zinc is a soft, silvery transition metal. Its main use is for **galvanizing**, which is a way of preventing steel objects from rusting by coating them with a thin layer of zinc. Zinc is also used in batteries and for making brass (which is an alloy of zinc and copper).

Poor metals

The remaining **metals** are in groups 3, 4, 5 and 6 of the periodic table, although each of these groups also contains **elements** that are **non-metals**, too. The metals appear on the right-hand side of the table (see page 41).

These metals are often called poor metals because they are much softer and weaker than the transition metals. They also have lower **melting** and **boiling points**. The most important of these metals are aluminium, tin and lead.

Aluminium

Aluminium is a silver-coloured metal. It is the most abundant metal in the rocks of the Earth's crust and has several useful **properties**. It is only about one third the **density** of steel, but just as strong when it is **alloyed** with small amounts of other metals. All large aircraft, and some cars and boats, are made from aluminium alloys. Aluminium is quite **reactive**, but its **oxide** is very unreactive. This means that a coating of oxide forms naturally on aluminium objects, which stops any further **corrosion**. Most aluminium is made into drinks cans and kitchen foil.

Tin

Tin is used to make a material called tin plate; this is steel with a thin layer of tin on one side. 'Tin' cans are made from tin plate, with the tin on the inside – next to the food. The tin stops the steel being corroded by the contents of the can.

Solder is an alloy of lead and tin. The soldering iron melts it easily. It turns quickly solid again, joining the wires together.

Lead

Lead is a very dense, grey metal. It is used in buildings for waterproofing because it does not corrode. Thick sheets of lead stop **radiation**, so it is also used to protect staff and patients in hospitals from **X-rays**. Lead used to be made into water pipes, but this was stopped because lead is poisonous and small amounts of it were carried from the pipes into drinking water.

Metalloids

Most elements have either the properties of metals or the properties of non-metals, although there are a few elements with some properties of both. They are called **metalloids** or semi-metals. An example is the metalloid arsenic, which is shiny like a metal, but does not **conduct** electricity or heat. Silicon is the most common metalloid – in fact, it is the second most common element on Earth. Pure silicon is hard, shiny and grey.

The most important use of metalloids is to make materials called semiconductors. A semiconductor is a material that can conduct some electricity (compared to an insulator) but not as well as metals, which are good conductors. This means it can be used to turn electric currents on and off. Microchips, often called silicon chips, are also made from silicon or other metalloids.

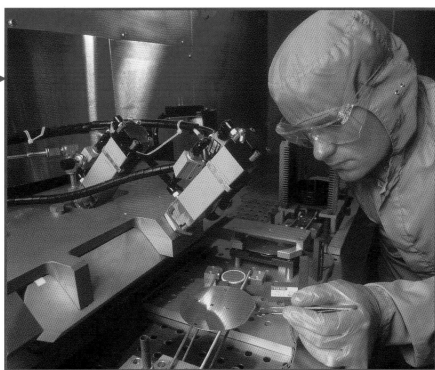

Silicon chips are made by building layers of semiconductors onto a wafer of silicon.

Metals in reactions

The most common reactions of **metals** are with air, water and **acids**.

Iron or steel objects that are left outdoors quickly go brown and flaky. This process is called rusting. The bright white flashes of fireworks are caused by magnesium in the fireworks burning. These are both examples of metals reacting with other substances.

Metals and the air

Most metals react with oxygen in the air, the metal combines with the oxygen to form a metal **oxide**. Here is an example of a metal reacting with oxygen:

$$\text{aluminium} + \text{oxygen} \longrightarrow \text{aluminium oxide}$$
$$4Al + 3O_2 \longrightarrow 2Al_2O_3$$

In this reaction, oxygen is added to the aluminium, it is an example of a type of reaction called an oxidation reaction. The aluminium is oxidized. The evidence that the reaction has happened is that the shininess on its surface disappears – this is called tarnishing. With aluminium, the aluminium oxide stops oxygen getting to the aluminium underneath, preventing further tarnishing.

Some metals react with cold air; an example is sodium, which is stored in oil because it tarnishes so quickly in the air. Some metals, such as magnesium, only react when they are heated, while others such as iron react only slowly, even when they are heated. Other metals, such as gold, don't react at all – they are completely unreactive.

Exposed calcium reacts quickly with oxygen in the air to form a layer of calcium oxide.

Experiment: Metal and air reactions

PROBLEM: Do common metals react with the air?

HYPOTHESIS: Everyday metals such as iron, copper and aluminium look shiny. They don't react with the air at room temperature, but they might when they are heated.

Experiment steps

EQUIPMENT
thin strands of copper wire
thin strands of iron wire or
    wire/steel wool
aluminium foil
tongs or a wooden peg

1 Cut a piece of aluminium kitchen foil about 30cm long and 1cm wide. Ask an adult to strip 5cm of insulation from some stranded copper wire and some stranded iron wire.

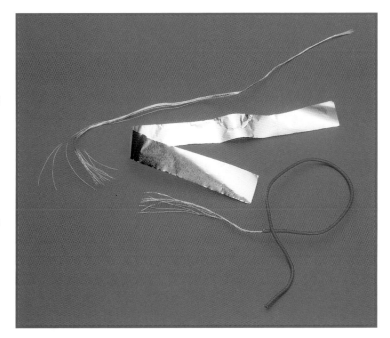

2 An adult must do this step for you. Ask them to heat the last centimetre of the foil in the flame of a gas cooker until it glows red hot. Then remove it from the heat. Do the same with the iron wire and copper wire.

3 Allow the metals to cool for a few minutes and examine the parts that you have heated.

CONCLUSION: Each metal is covered with a layer of a new substance. This is probably an oxide of the metal, formed by the reaction of the metal with oxygen in the air. Aluminium reacted most quickly, then iron and then copper.

Metals and acids

Most **metals** react with **acids**. When a piece of metal is put in an acid, the metal fizzes because gas is formed. The gas is hydrogen, which is released from the acid, and the metal combines with the rest of the acid to make a chemical called a **salt**. Here is an example of an acid-metal reaction:

magnesium	+	sulfuric acid	⟶	hydrogen	+	magnesium sulfate
Mg	+	H_2SO_4	⟶	H_2	+	$MgSO_4$

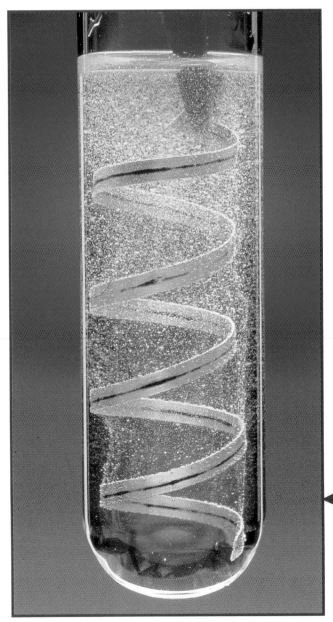

The metal pushes out, or displaces, the hydrogen from the acid, so this is an example of a reaction called a **displacement reaction**.

When different metals are added to acids, the fizzing happens at different speeds. When **reactive** metals, such as potassium, are added to acid, the reaction is so fast that the metal explodes. With other metals, such as magnesium, the fizzing does happen quickly but not explosively. When metals such as iron are added to acids, the fizzing happens slowly, and some metals, such as gold, don't react with acids at all.

Magnesium ribbon reacting with hydrochloric acid, producing bubbles of hydrogen.

Experiment: Reactions of metals and acids

PROBLEM: How can we remove the zinc from a galvanized steel nail?

HYPOTHESIS: Zinc reacts with acids better than steel, it might react with a weak acid, forming a salt, leaving the steel behind. Vinegar contains a weak acid called acetic acid, so putting the nail in vinegar should work.

EQUIPMENT
galvanized steel nail
white vinegar
glass jar

Experiment steps

1 Pour 1cm of vinegar into a glass jar. Vinegar is a weak acid, so be careful not to splash any in your eyes. Drop in a galvanized steel nail, and look at the nail every half an hour to see what is happening.

2 Wash the nail when the fizzing has stopped.

CONCLUSION: After a few minutes the nail begins to fizz. This fizzing is hydrogen being formed by the reaction between the zinc and the acid. When the fizzing stops, all the zinc has reacted and a plain steel nail is left.

Metals and water

Some **metals** react with water. When a piece of one of these metals is put in water, it fizzes because a gas is formed. The gas is hydrogen, which is released from the water. The metal combines with the hydrogen and oxygen in the water to make a hydroxide, this makes the **solution** alkaline. Here is an example of a metal-water reaction:

sodium + water   ⟶   sodium + hydrogen
hydroxide

$$2Na + 2H_2O \longrightarrow 2NaOH + H_2$$

Some metals, such as potassium, react violently with water, and this reaction makes enough heat to ignite the hydrogen gas. Some metals, such as magnesium, react slowly with water, and others, such as copper, do not react with water at all. Some metals that don't react quickly with water, such as iron, will react with steam to make an **oxide** and water.

A piece of potassium reacting with water.

The reactivity series

Different metals react with air, water and acids at different speeds. In each reaction the **reactant** and **products** are similar, but some metals react quickly while others react slowly. This is an example of a **trend**; it is always the same metals that react quickly and the same metals that react slowly.

We can list common metals in order of how quickly they react, with the ones that react most quickly at the top. The order is the same for reactions with air, water and acids, and chemists call the list the reactivity series. Here is the reactivity series of common metals:

Metal	Symbol	Reactivity
potassium	K	Most reactive
sodium	Na	
calcium	Ca	
magnesium	Mg	
aluminium	Al	
zinc	Zn	
iron	Fe	
lead	Pb	
copper	Cu	
silver	Ag	
gold	Au	Least reactive

The reactivity series helps us to work out what might happen during some **chemical reactions**. For example, a metal higher in the series will displace a metal lower in the series from a **compound**, like this:

copper + magnesium $\longrightarrow$ magnesium + copper
sulfate   sulfate
$CuSO_4$ + Mg $\longrightarrow$ $MgSO_4$ + Cu

Hydrogen is often included in the reactivity series. Acids, which contain hydrogen, react with metals higher in the series, but they do not react with metals lower in the series. In the series above, hydrogen would be between lead and copper.

Corrosion

Corrosion is caused by a reaction between a **metal** and oxygen in the air, and sometimes water or water vapour, too. We normally use the word corrosion when the reaction spoils and weakens the metal. Some metals, such as iron and steel, corrode quickly in damp air, whereas others such as gold, don't corrode at all because they are very unreactive. Some metals, such as aluminium and zinc, do react with the air, but they do not corrode. This is because the metal **oxide** layer made by the reaction protects the metal underneath. This is why zinc and aluminium are used to make or cover objects that are outdoors.

Rusting

The most common form of corrosion is rusting, which is the corrosion of iron and steel when they react with oxygen and water. The flaky, red-brown rust is called iron oxide, and it crumbles away, allowing the metal underneath to rust, too. Here is the equation for the reaction that makes rust:

$$\text{iron} + \text{oxygen} \longrightarrow \text{iron oxide}$$
$$4Fe + 3O_2 \longrightarrow 2Fe_2O_3$$

The steel body of this van is gradually rusting away.

Preventing rusting

Rusting of steel is an expensive problem, so preventing it is important. The easiest way of stopping rusting is to cover the steel to stop air and water reaching it. This can be done with paint, plastic, grease or another metal that does not corrode, such as zinc. Covering steel with zinc is called **galvanization**.

Experiment: What causes rusting?

PROBLEM: What causes iron and steel objects to rust?

HYPOTHESIS: Iron or steel objects rust when they are left outdoors, but not when they are inside, so it is probably water or air, or both, that cause rusting.

EQUIPMENT
steel nails (about 5cm long)
4 glass jars
cling film
calcium chloride (if available)
oil (such as cooking oil)
boiled water

Experiment steps

1 Stand four glass jars in a row and number them from 1 to 4. Drop a steel nail into each jar.

2 Pour 2cm of tap water into jar 1.

3 Fill jar 2 to the brim with water that has been boiled, by an adult, to remove dissolved air (and cooled) and cover it with cling film. The cling film will stop air re-dissolving in the water.

Jar 1   Jar 2   Jar 3   Jar 4

4 Put a few lumps of calcium chloride in jar 3. This will keep the air in the jar dry. If no calcium chloride is available leave the jar empty, and put some cling film over the top to stop damp air getting in.

5 Fill jar 4 with oil so that it covers the nail.

6 Observe the jars each day for three days and write down what has happened to each nail in each jar.

CONCLUSION: Only the nail exposed to air and water (jar 1) rusts. We can conclude that rusting happens only when steel nails are exposed to both air and water.

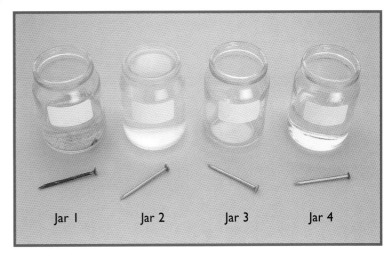
Jar 1   Jar 2   Jar 3   Jar 4

Finding metals

All the different **metals** you see in ornaments, tools, furniture, buildings and machines come from rocks that form the Earth's crust. Before we can use metals, we have to find the rocks that contain them, dig them out and then **extract** the metals from them. Some metals are abundant. For example, aluminium, the most abundant metal, makes up seven per cent of the Earth's crust. Others are very rare, such as gold which makes up only 0.000 000 5 per cent of the Earth's crust!

Metal	Percentage of Earth's crust	Date discovered
aluminium	7	1825
sodium	2.5	1807
magnesium	2	1755
zinc	0.007	2000 years ago
iron	4	3000 years ago
tin	0.0002	6000 years ago
lead	0.0015	6500 years ago
copper	0.0045	7000 years ago
gold	0.000 000 5	10 000 years ago

This table shows the percentage of the Earth's crust made up by the most common metals.

Metal ores

Most metals are found in **compounds**, which are often metal **oxides**. These compounds are called **ores** and they are normally mixed with other compounds in the rocks. Mining companies find the rocks by carrying out **geological surveys**. After the rocks are mined they are crushed; ready for the metals to be extracted.

Very unreactive metals such as gold are not locked up in compounds; they are called **native metals** and are often found in rocks as lumps called nuggets.

Extracting metals from ores

Metals are extracted from their ores using **chemical reactions**. In a reaction to extract a metal from its ore, the ore is one of the **reactants** and the metal is one of the **products**. The higher in the reactivity series the metal is, the more difficult it is to extract from its ore, and so the more expensive it is to produce and to buy.

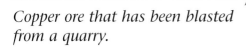

Copper ore that has been blasted from a quarry.

Discovering metals

The discovery of different common metals through the ages is closely linked to the reactivity series. Gold and silver do not react easily and so are often found as elements (not combined in compounds) and they were discovered more than ten thousand years ago. Copper was discovered next because it is only slightly reactive and can be extracted from its ore easily. From about five thousand years ago, bronze, an **alloy** of copper and tin, was used to make weapons and ornaments. Iron, which is more **reactive** than copper, was discovered next, before Roman times. Aluminium is very reactive and so it is difficult to extract from its ore. Ancient people did not even know it existed, and it was not extracted until 1825, when the electricity supplies needed for electrolysis (see page 34) became available.

Extraction reactions

The main methods of **extracting metals** from their **ores** are: decomposition, electrolysis and displacement. In each case some energy must be supplied to break up the ore into its **elements**. All the methods of extracting metals from their ores are also known as smelting. For example, iron smelting is a process for getting iron from iron ore.

Decomposition

A decomposition reaction is a reaction in which a **compound** splits up to make two or more different elements or more simple compounds. Thermal decomposition is decomposition that happens when a material is heated. Mercury is extracted from mercury **oxide** by thermal decomposition. Mercury oxide is a red powder, which **decomposes** on heating to make liquid mercury metal and oxygen gas.

$$\text{mercury oxide} \longrightarrow \text{mercury} + \text{oxygen}$$
$$2HgO \longrightarrow 2Hg + O_2$$

Thermal decomposition only works for metals that are quite unreactive. The ores of more **reactive** metals, such as iron and copper, would have to be heated to an extremely high temperature to make them decompose.

Heated mercury oxide decomposing. You can see mercury metal forming on the side of the test tube.

Displacement

When a reactive metal reacts with the compound of a less reactive metal, the more reactive metal can displace (push out) the less reactive metal from the compound. The more reactive metal forms a new compound, and the less reactive metal is left on its own. These reactions are called displacement reactions. For example, if iron filings are added to a **solution** of copper sulfate, the iron (which is more reactive than copper) displaces the copper. Iron sulfate and copper metal are formed as a result.

$$\text{iron} + \text{copper sulfate} \longrightarrow \text{iron sulfate} + \text{copper}$$

$$Fe + CuSO_4 \longrightarrow FeSO_4 + Cu$$

A displacement reaction in progress. Copper is displacing the silver in silver nitrate solution, leaving silver metal.

Electrolysis

Electrolysis is a way of splitting a **compound** into its **elements** using electricity. It is used to **decompose ores** that would need to be heated to extremely high temperatures before they would decompose. Aluminium, magnesium and sodium are all extracted from their ores by electrolysis.

Electrolysis can only happen to a substance that contains **charged particles** called ions. If an **atom** loses **electrons** it becomes a positively charged ion, and if an atom gains electrons it becomes a negatively charged ion. The substance must also be **molten** to make a liquid, or dissolved in a liquid to make a **solution**, because the ions must be free to move about.

To make electrolysis happen two electrical contacts, called **electrodes**, are put into the liquid and then connected to a supply of electricity. This makes ions with a positive charge move through the liquid to one electrode, and ions with a negative charge move to the other electrode. When the ions reach the electrodes they turn back into atoms.

Electrolysis in progress at an aluminium smelting plant.

Extracting aluminium

The main ore of aluminium is called bauxite and it contains aluminium **oxide**. Aluminium is very **reactive**, so it does not decompose when it is heated. This means it must be **extracted** by electrolysis.

First, the bauxite is processed to get crystals of pure aluminium oxide, called alumina. Alumina melts at a very high temperature, which would be expensive, so it is dissolved at a lower temperature in a molten substance called cryolite. The mixture of alumina and cryolite is put into a container called a cell. The cell is lined with graphite, which forms one of the electrodes. The other electrode, also made of graphite, dips into the mixture from the top. When electricity is passed through the mixture, aluminium ions are attracted to the graphite lining and they turn into aluminium atoms. These atoms group together to form molten aluminium, and this is piped off and cooled to form the finished **metal**.

Cheap aluminium

Scientists first extracted aluminium in the early 19th century, but only in tiny amounts, and the cost was very high. At the time aluminium was in short supply and more expensive than gold.

The most important breakthrough in the extraction of aluminium was the invention of the dynamo – a machine that produces electricity. This allowed power stations to be built, providing the electricity needed for the electrolysis of aluminium oxide.

Two scientists, the American Charles Hall and the Frenchman Paul-Louis-Toussaint Héroult, both developed a method of producing aluminium by electrolysis in 1886. Soon aluminium was available in large amounts, and was much cheaper than gold.

The iron and steel industry

Iron is the cheapest and most useful **metal** in the world, and steel is its most important **alloy**. Iron-making and steel-making are two of the world's largest industries, and hundreds of millions of tonnes of steel are made every year. Here you can find out how iron is **extracted** from its **ore** and turned into steel.

Smelting iron

Iron is extracted from its ore, iron **oxide**, in a very hot furnace called a blast furnace. Iron oxide and coke (which is almost pure carbon) are put into the top of the furnace, and air is blasted into the base of the furnace. The coke does two jobs. Firstly, it burns in the air, heating the furnace to 1500°C. Secondly, because carbon is more **reactive** than iron, it displaces the iron from the iron oxide. Here's the equation for the reaction:

$$\text{carbon} + \text{iron oxide} \longrightarrow \text{carbon dioxide} + \text{iron}$$
$$3C + 2Fe_2O_3 \longrightarrow 3CO_2 + 4Fe$$

The **molten** iron flows to the bottom of the furnace and through pipes to be collected. It is then put in moulds and cooled. The iron from the blast furnace is called pig iron. It contains up to ten per cent carbon, which makes it very brittle.

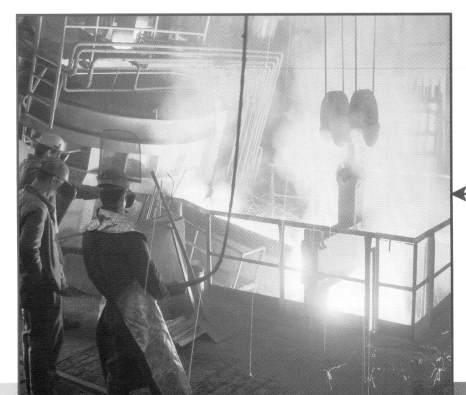

The scene at a blast furnace. Huge vats of molten metal are handled by remote control.

Iron to steel

Steel is iron that contains about one per cent carbon. Iron from a blast furnace is made into steel in a furnace called a basic oxygen furnace. Molten iron is poured into the furnace, then jets of pure oxygen are blown into the iron. The oxygen reacts with the carbon producing carbon dioxide that is removed from the furnace. This reduces the amount of carbon in the iron and so produces steel. The furnace is tipped up and the steel pours into moulds to cool. A large steel-making plant can make up to ten million tonnes of steel a year, which is enough to make a thousand big car ferries.

Henry Bessemer (1813–98)

British engineer Henry Bessemer invented the modern steel-making process in the middle of the 19th century. He realized that blowing air through molten iron would remove the carbon from the iron, making steel. Before this, steel was a rare and expensive metal but afterwards it became cheap and the most widely used metal of all.

Working with metals

The **metal** made in most production plants is poured into moulds to make lumps called **ingots**. In a steel works, the steel is fed into a machine that shapes it into sheets or bars. This is called continuous casting. Ingots, bars and sheets of metal are the **raw materials** for making all sorts of objects.

Casting, forging and rolling

Casting, forging and rolling are the three main methods of making pieces of metal into different shapes. In casting, the metal is heated until it melts and then poured into a mould. Inside the mould is a hole the same shape as the object to be cast. The hole fills with metal, which cools to form the object. In forging, the metal is heated until it glows red hot, but not enough to melt it. This makes it more **malleable**, and it can then be pressed or hammered into shape by machines or by hand tools.

In rolling, slabs of metal travel through a series of rollers that gradually flatten them into thin sheets, or bend them round into tubes. Blocks of metal can also be made into shapes with various cutting tools.

A blacksmith bends and shapes iron by heating it and hitting it with a hammer. This is called forging.

Joining metals

Pieces of metals can be joined together by welding and soldering. In one method of welding, the edges of the pieces are heated until they are so hot that they fuse together. In soldering, used in electronics and plumbing, an **alloy** called solder is melted so that it flows into the gap between the metals, bonds to them and joins them together.

Making metal coatings

Many metal objects have a thin coating of another metal on their surfaces. Cutlery is often silver-plated, which means it is made of steel with a coating of silver on the outside. Jewellery and ornaments are often gold-plated instead of being solid gold. Metal coatings are normally applied by electrolysis.

Metal recycling

Many metals can be recycled, which means that metal in old or worn-out objects is made into new objects. Recycling does not only save more metal **ore** being dug from the ground, the energy that would have been used to extract the metal from the ore is also saved – which is often more important.

Aluminium cans waiting to be recycled.

Metal fatigue

Metal fatigue happens when a piece of metal changes shape a tiny amount, again and again. This weakens the metal and eventually makes it break. Metal fatigue is a big problem in machines where metal parts, such as springs, are stretched or bent again and again. It is difficult to detect and often parts break suddenly, so it is important that parts of machines such as aircraft are checked regularly for the microscopic cracks that are a sign of metal fatigue.

The periodic table

The periodic table is a chart of all the known **elements**. The elements are arranged in order of their atomic numbers, but in rows, so that elements with similar **properties** are underneath each other. The periodic table gets its name from the fact that the properties the elements have repeat themselves every few elements, or periodically. The position of an element in the periodic table gives an idea of what its properties are likely to be.

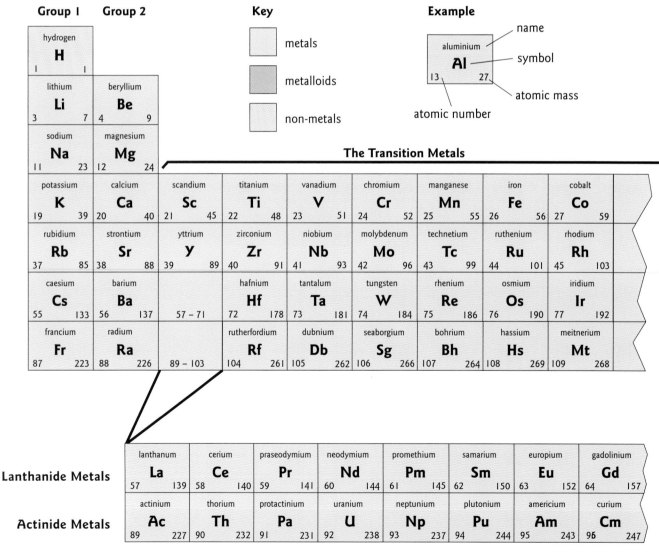

Groups and periods

The vertical columns of elements are called groups. The horizontal rows of elements are called periods. Some groups have special names:

Group 1: Alkali **metals**

Group 2: Alkaline earth metals

Group 7: Halogens

Group 0: Noble gases

The table is divided into two main sections, the metals and **non-metals**. Between the two are elements that have some properties of metals and some of non-metals. They are called semi-metals or **metalloids**.

			Group 3	Group 4	Group 5	Group 6	Group 7	Group 0
								helium **He** 2 4
			boron **B** 5 11	carbon **C** 6 12	nitrogen **N** 7 14	oxygen **O** 8 16	fluorine **F** 9 19	neon **Ne** 10 20
			aluminium **Al** 13 27	silicon **Si** 14 28	phosphorus **P** 15 31	sulfur **S** 16 32	chlorine **Cl** 17 35	argon **Ar** 18 40
nickel **Ni** 28 59	copper **Cu** 29 64	zinc **Zn** 30 65	gallium **Ga** 31 70	germanium **Ge** 32 73	arsenic **As** 33 75	selenium **Se** 34 79	bromine **Br** 35 80	krypton **Kr** 36 84
palladium **Pd** 46 106	silver **Ag** 47 108	cadmium **Cd** 48 112	indium **In** 49 115	tin **Sn** 50 119	antimony **Sb** 51 122	tellurium **Te** 52 128	iodine **I** 53 127	xenon **Xe** 54 131
platinum **Pt** 78 195	gold **Au** 79 197	mercury **Hg** 80 201	thallium **Tl** 81 204	lead **Pb** 82 207	bismuth **Bi** 83 209	polonium **Po** 84 209	astatine **At** 85 210	radon **Rn** 86 222
ununnilium **Uun** 110 271	unununium **Uuu** 111 272	ununbium **Uub** 112 285		ununquadium **Uuq** 114 289				

terbium **Tb** 65 159	dysprosium **Dy** 66 163	holmium **Ho** 67 165	erbium **Er** 68 167	thulium **Tm** 69 169	ytterbium **Yb** 70 173	lutetium **Lu** 71 175
berkelium **Bk** 97 247	californium **Cf** 98 251	einsteinium **Es** 99 252	fermium **Fm** 100 257	mendelevium **Md** 101 258	nobelium **No** 102 259	lawrencium **Lr** 103 262

Common metals and metalloids

These are some of the **melting** and **boiling points** for pure **metals** and **metalloids** that occur in the periodic table.

Metal	Symbol	State at room temperature	Melting pt (°C)	Boiling pt (°C)
lithium	Li	solid	180	1342
sodium	Na	solid	98	883
magnesium	Mg	solid	650	1090
aluminium	Al	solid	660	2519
silicon	Si	solid	1414	2900
potassium	K	solid	63	759
calcium	Ca	solid	842	1487
iron	Fe	solid	1535	2861
copper	Cu	solid	1083	2595
zinc	Zn	solid	420	907
silver	Ag	solid	961	2210
tin	Sn	solid	232	2270
gold	Au	solid	1063	2970
mercury	Hg	liquid	-39	357
lead	Pb	solid	327	1744

The reactivity series

The reactivity series is a list of common metals in order of their reactivity, together with their reactions with air, water and **acid**. The most **reactive** metals are at the top and least reactive at the bottom.

Metal	Symbol	Air	Water	Acid
potassium	K	Burns easily	Reacts with cold water	Violent reaction
sodium	Na	Burns easily	Reacts with cold water	Violent reaction
calcium	Ca	Burns easily	Reacts with cold water	Violent reaction
magnesium	Mg	Burns easily	Reacts with steam	Very reactive
aluminium	Al	Reacts slowly	Reacts with steam	Very reactive
zinc	Zn	Reacts slowly	Reacts with steam	Quite reactive
iron	Fe	Reacts slowly	Reacts with steam	Quite reactive
lead	Pb	Reacts slowly	Reacts slowly with steam	Reacts very slowly
copper	Cu	Reacts slowly	No reaction	No reaction
silver	Ag	No reaction	No reaction	No reaction
gold	Au	No reaction	No reaction	No reaction

Glossary of technical terms

acid liquid that is sour to taste, that can eat away metals and is neutralized by alkalis and bases. Acids have a pH below 7.

alkali liquid with a pH above 7. Alkalis feel soapy and slimy.

alloy material made by mixing a metal with another metal or a small amount of a non-metal. For example, steel is an alloy of iron and carbon.

atom extremely tiny particle of matter. The smallest particle of an element that can exist, and which has the properties of that element. All substances are made up of atoms.

boiling point temperature at which a substance changes state from liquid to gas

bond chemical join or connection between two atoms, ions or molecules

catalyst chemical that makes a chemical reaction happen faster but is unchanged at the end of the reaction

charge electricity on an object, such as an atom or electron

chemical reaction happens when two chemicals (called the reactants) react together to form new chemicals (called the products)

compound substance that contains two or more different elements joined together by chemical bonds

conductor material that allows electricity (an electrical conductor) or heat (a heat conductor) to pass through it easily

corrosion any chemical reaction that eats away a material, such as rusting

decompose turn into more simple chemicals

density the amount of a substance (or mass) in a certain volume. Density is measured in grams per cubic centimetre or kilograms per cubic metre.

ductile describes a material that can be pulled into a thin wire without breaking. Metals are ductile.

electrode solid electrical conductor, usually graphite or metal, that is in contact with the liquid in electrolysis

electron extremely tiny particle that is part of an atom. Electrons are negatively charged, and they move around the nucleus of an atom.

element substance that contains just one type of atom. An element cannot be changed into simpler substances.

extract remove a substance from a mixture of substances

galvanizing coating iron or steel objects with a layer of zinc to stop them rusting

geological survey an investigation to find out what layers of rocks are under the ground in a particular place

ingot piece of pure metal, such as gold, made by pouring molten metal into a mould

magnetic describes a material that is attracted to a magnet or can be turned into a magnet itself.

malleable describes a material that can be hammered into shape without breaking. All metals are malleable.

melting point temperature at which a substance changes state from a solid to a liquid as it warms up

metal any element in the periodic table that is shiny, and that conducts electricity and heat well. Most metals are also hard.

metalloid element that cannot be classed as a metal or a non-metal. It has some of the properties of a metal and some of the properties of a non-metal.

mixture substance made up of two or more elements or compounds that are not joined together by chemical bonds

molten describes a substance that has been heated until it melts

native metal metal that is found as an element in the Earth's crust, such as gold, rather than as part of a compound

non-metal any element in the periodic table that is not a metal. Most non-metals are gases.

nucleus central part of an atom

neutron one of the particles that makes up the nucleus of an atom. Neutrons are not electrically charged.

ore material dug from the ground that contains useful elements, such as iron, aluminium or sulfur

oxide compound made up of a metal or non-metal combined with oxygen, such as aluminium oxide or carbon dioxide

particle very tiny piece of a substance, such as a single atom, ion or molecule

product substance formed during a chemical reaction

properties characteristics of a chemical, such as colour, feel and density

proton one of the particles that makes up the nucleus of an atom. Protons are positively charged.

radioactive describes a substance that gives off radiation

radiation rays, such as light and heat, or streams of particles

raw material simple material that is made into more complex materials or objects

reactant substance that takes part in a chemical reaction

reactive describes a chemical that takes part in chemical reactions easily

solution liquid made when a substance (the solute) dissolves in a liquid (the solvent)

trend the general direction of change in a property

X-ray form of radiation that passes through some substances (such as flesh) but not others (such as bone)

Further reading

Chemical Chaos (Horrible Science)
Nick Arnold, Tony de Saulles, Scholastic Hippo, 1997

Chemicals in Action
Ann Fullick, Heinemann Library, 1999

Co-ordinated Science, Chemistry Foundation
Andy Bethell, John Dexter, Mike Griffths, Heinemann, 2001

The Dorling Kindersley Science Encyclopedia
Dorling Kindersley, 1993

How Science Works
Judith Hann, Dorling Kindersley, 1991

The Usborne Illustrated Dictionary of Chemistry
Jane Wertheim, Chris Oxlade and Dr. John Waterhouse
Usborne, 1987

Useful websites

http://www.heinemannexplore.com
An exciting new online resource for school libraries and classrooms containing articles, investigations, biographies and activities related to all areas of the science curriculum.

http://www.creative-chemistry.org.uk
An interactive chemistry site including fun practical activities, worksheets, quizzes, puzzles and more! With links to many more useful and interesting sites including:

http://www.bbc.co.uk/science
Loads of information on all areas of science. Includes news, activities, games and quizzes.

http://www.chemicool.com
All you ever needed to know about the elements – and more!

http://www.webelements.com/webelements/scholar
The Periodic table – online! Discover more about all the elements and their properties.

http://particleadventure.org
An interactive site, explaining the fundamentals of matter and forces!

Disclaimer
All the Internet addresses (URLs) given in this book were valid at the time of going to press. However, due to the dynamic nature of the Internet, some addresses may have changed, or sites may have ceased to exist since publication. While the author and publishers regret any inconvenience this may cause readers, no responsibility for any such changes can be accepted by either the author or the publishers.

Index